To mum
Happy chistmas

CW00431481

xxx

EASY TO MAKE
FLOWER ARRANGING

EASY TO MAKE

FLOWER ARRANGING

Mary Lawrence

ANAYA PUBLISHERS LTD LONDON

First published in Great Britain in 1992
by Anaya Publishers Ltd, Strode House,
44–50 Osnaburgh Street, London NW1 3ND

All text by Mary Lawrence except on
pages 110–111 where text by Kerrie Dudley

Editor Eve Harlow
Designed by Design 23
Photographer Richard Paines
Illustrator Coral Mula

British Library Cataloguing in Publication Data

Lawrence, Mary
Flower arranging. – (Easy to make)
1. Handicrafts.
I. Title II Series
ISBN 1-85470-116-9

Typeset by Servis Filmsetting Ltd, Manchester, UK
Colour reproduction by Columbia Offset, Singapore
Printed and bound in Portugal by
Resopal Industria Grafica Lda

Contents

Introduction

There is a strong creative urge in most of us and flower arrangers are fortunate in having one of the most beautiful mediums in the world with which to use their creative skills.

Although I have worked with flowers all my life, my creative urge is undiminished and my imagination still goes into 'fast forward' when I look at flowers and see a good colour combination, or come upon a beautifully shaped branch of blossom or even discover an unusual container.

One of the best things about flower arranging is that one never stops learning. I still come to arranging flowers with a fresh and open approach and a sense of excitement, whether it is a grand display for an important venue or a small table centre for my home.

When I ran my own flower shop I had to be in the flower market at 4.30am, but it was no hardship, for the riot of colour and the beauty of hundreds of thousands of blooms lifted my spirits very high. Seeing anemones that, a few hours earlier, had been growing in Italy, mimosa from the south of France, lilacs and tulips from Holland and proteas and orchids from Australia, I always felt as if I had had a world trip before most people had eaten their breakfast! Nothing could take away the joy of working with flowers.

Nowadays, flowers can be bought in all kinds of places and almost at any time of day. With cheaper air freight, beautiful flowers and foliage come fresh from virtually all parts of the world, giving us an unrivalled choice.

In recent years there has been a decline in the rigid, symmetrical approach to flower designing and a return to the free-style flower arranging first encouraged by the English landscape gardener, Gertrude Jekyll, in the late 19th and early 20th centuries.

Free-style flower arranging allows a person's individuality to have full rein and not be fenced in with rules. It is not, after all, a technical exercise but an art form; so much depends on each person's eye, the materials available and the ambience that is to be created.

In this book, I have created a varied selection of arrangements that I hope you will find easy. I have listed the materials used, the method and order in which I have worked but I also hope that I have left you the freedom to incorporate some of your own ideas into the designs.

If you study my approach you will see graceful lines and outlines that flow and give shape to the arrangement. You will see a balance and harmony in the proportions of the displays and I hope that you can observe a new insight in the colour combinations I have used.

Whether you are using this book as a beginner who will find the basic information enlightening or as an experienced flower arranger who would like to try something different, it is my hope that you will share my sense of excitement when you are re-creating some of my designs.

Years ago, I was told by Constance Spry, doyenne of English flower arranging, that the most important things to remember when creating flower pictures were Colour, Line and Proportion. I always add another very important word – Imagination.

ONE

Table Centres

Fresh spring arrangement

This unusual design is arranged on a cheese dish with the cover forming an integral part of the colour scheme. As the anemones and tulips open, the arrangement will change its shape and the blue throatwort will deepen in colour.

Materials
Cheese dish and lid
Green florist's foam, soaked
Plastic pin holder
Adhesive clay tape

Fresh flowers
Silver dollar eucalyptus *Eucalyptus cinera*
Cerise anemones *Anemone coronoria*
Mauve tulips *Tulipa*
Blue throatwort *Trachelium caeruleum*

Preparation
1 Fix the soaked foam block on to the pin holder and secure the cheese dish with clay tape.

2 Position the cheese dish cover at an angle supported on the foam block at the back.

The plants used in the arrangement are: eucalyptus (1) anemones (2) eucalyptus (3) anemones (4) tulips (5) throatwort (6).

Working the design

3 Take a stem of eucalyptus twice the height of the dish and cover and push it into the foam so that it leans over and follows the line of the cover.

4 Insert the anemones in graduating height to follow the line of the cover.

5 Use more eucalyptus to build the outline of the arrangement. Place a further group of anemones so that they rest over the edge of the dish.

6 Position the tulips so that they form a focal point (see picture).

7 Fill in the arrangement with blue throatwort.

The botanical name for throatwort is *Trachelium caeruleum*, from the Greek 'trachea' meaning 'throat'. This plant is said to have been used to treat neck and throat aches.

11

Pot-et-fleur

Arrangements of cut flowers and growing plants are an ideal combination when flowers are in short supply and you can keep an arrangement going for several months by changing the cut flower part of the design.

Materials
Deep tureen (or similar container)
Potting compost
Glass jar packed with wire netting
Bun or carpet moss
Florist's pins

Flowers and plants
Hyacinth bulbs, blue *Hyacinthus orientalis*
Begonia plant *Begonia rex*
Polyanthus plant (pink) *Primula variabillis*
Cut spray chrysanthemums (pink)
    Chrysanthemum hybrid

Preparation
1 Place some broken pieces of flower pot or stones in the container.

2 Keeping the lid on the jar, sink it into the broken pottery at the back of the container.

Working the design
3 Lift the plants from their pots, retaining the soil ball.

> To keep the water in the jar fresh, place the container by the sink and pour in water until the jar overflows and all the water is renewed. A small piece of charcoal added to the water will help to keep it odourless.

4 Put a little compost in the container and position the plants.

5 Now fill the container with compost, packing it in tightly.

6 Clean the outside and rim of the container if necessary and cover the surface with moss, securing it with florist's pins (see Better Techniques).

7 Remove the lid, pour fresh water in the jar and arrange the chrysanthemums.

Place broken crocks in the container, position the growing hyacinth.

Mixed pink arrangement

These beautifully marked lilies originated in America but the bulbs are now mainly cultivated in Holland and the flowers exported all over the world. The lilies have a lovely fragrance and they make a striking focal point in this mixed pink arrangement.

Materials
Round vase
Plastic pin holder
Adhesive clay tape
Green florist's foam soaked

Fresh flowers
Pink lilies *Lilium orientalis*
Pink broom *Cytisus*
Pink gladioli *Gladiolus*
White rose *Rosa*
Laurustinus *Laurustinus*
Variegated ivy *Hedera helix*

Preparation
1 Cut the foam to fit into the vase so that about 1in (2.5cm) stands above the rim.

2 Secure the foam in the vase (refer to Better Techniques).

Working the design
3 Place the lilies from the back to the middle to build height.

4 Place ivy to fall over the edge of the vase to soften the line.

5 Arange the gladioli so that they give weight at the sides.

6 Position the roses through the centre front.

7 Fill in the arrangement with laurustinus and broom to break up any hard lines.

Lilies (1) ivy (2) gladioli (3) roses (4).

It is important to pick or trim off *Lilium orientalis* anthers before they pollinate, as the pollen will stain any surface it falls upon.
   It is a good idea to remove one of the lily florets from a heavily-flowered stem. It will make little difference to your arrangement but the handsome, single flower can be displayed in a specimen vase.

Arrangement on a plate

For this simple yet striking arrangement you need a beautiful plate or shallow bowl and a few preserved leaves and flowers. Placed on a low table in a hallway or near to a door, it will make for a dramatic entrance.

Materials
Deep plate or shallow bowl
'Staysoft' (florist's modelling clay)
Adhesive clay tape
Silver stub wires

Preserved leaves and flowers
Oak leaves *Quercus robur*
Peony head *Paeonia lactiflora*
Dahlias *Dahlia*
Sprays of bleached hair-grass *Aira sp.*

Preparation
1 Secure a small ball of 'Staysoft', off-centre, to the plate with a strip of clay tape.

Different preserving techniques have been used for the plants in this arrangement. The oak leaves were preserved in a glycerine solution, the peony was preserved in silica gel and the dahlias were air-dried.
  Hair-grass can be bleached by resting sprays in a weak solution of domestic bleach overnight.

2 Wire the oak leaves (see Better Techniques) and insert them into the 'Staysoft' to form a flat, assymetrical arrangement.

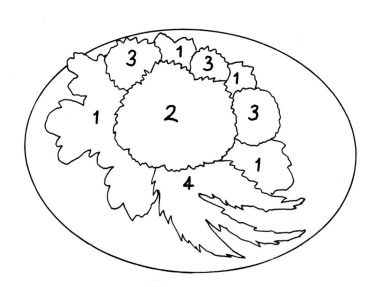

Oak leaves (1) peony head (2) dahlias (3) hair-grass (4).

Working the design
3 Position the peony in the centre.

4 Arrange the dahlias under the edges of the peony.

5 Tuck a few stems of the hair-grass under the peony head to follow the lines of the plate.

This design can also be made with fresh flowers using broken-off blossoms that would otherwise be discarded – roses, camellias, florets of gladiola and azaleas. If the heads are floated in shallow water they will last a short time.

17

Victorian posy

This kind of arrangement is the perfect shape for displaying on a low table as it is best viewed from above. Although the posy is easy to make, the precise positioning of each flower to produce the formal shape takes time and patience.

DRIED FLOWER POSY
Materials
Small, round tureen or bowl
Brown florist's foam
Plastic pin holder
Adhesive clay tape
Black reel wire

Dried flowers
Single helichrysum *Helichrysum*
Broom bloom, bleached
Hill flowers, coral coloured
Blue delphinium *Delphinium elatum*
Achillea, coral coloured *Achillea*
Reed canary grass (dyed coral) *Phalaris*

Preparation
1 Cut the foam to fit the bowl and secure it, leaving 2in (5cm) over the edge.

2 Use a sharp knife to cut the protruding foam into a dome shape.

3 Cut the broom bloom into short lengths and wire into small bunches, leaving 2 legs (see Better Techniques).

4 Mount single florets of delphinium.

Working the design
5 Position the helichrysum in the centre of the foam.

6 Cut stems of reed canary grass to 2in (5cm) long and insert them into the foam around the rim of the bowl, positoning them to make a tight circle.

7 Make a circle of wired broom blooms interspersed with hill flowers round the central flower.

8 Next, insert a tight circle of delphinium florets.

9 Follow this with a circle of achillea, positioning the flower heads towards the outer circle. Fill in the remaining gap with broom blooms and hill flowers to form the finished dome-shaped posy.

FRESH FLOWER POSY
Materials
Small, round tureen or bowl
Wire netting; securing tape

Fresh flowers
Primroses and leaves *Primula*
Cream-coloured rose *Rosa*
Forget-me-nots *Myosotis*

Preparation
1 Crumple the wire netting into the container and secure with tape.

Working the design
2 Take a quantity of primrose leaves and trim the bottom 1in (2.5cm) from each side of the stem, leaving the stem bare.

3 Position the leaves to overlap the edge of the container to give a circular outline.

4 Position the rose in the centre of the bowl, standing at a height of half the diameter of the bowl. Surround the rose with a tight circle of forget-me-nots, then a circle of primroses.

5 Continue adding alternate circles of forget-me-nots and primroses until the centre is filled in.

TWO

Love Stories

Basket of dried flowers

A lasting gift of dried flowers prettily arranged in a basket to show a mother how much she is loved. Paper ribbon has been used to decorate the basket and is the perfect texture to use with dried flowers.

Materials
Basket painted in a pastel shade
Brown florist's foam
Florist's securing tape
Paper ribbon in two shades
Clear all-purpose adhesive

Dried flowers
Hydrangea heads *Hydrangea macrophylla*
Wild oats, dyed maroon *Avena Fatua*
Larkspur *Delphinium Consolida*
Helichrysum *Helichrysum Bracteatum*

Preparation
1 Cut the foam to fit the basket and secure with tape.

Working the design
2 Break the hydrangea into manageable florets and pin into the foam to make a bed of hydrangeas but leaving the centre clear.

3 Divide the dried wild oats and wire them into small bunches of various sizes.

Hydrangea florets (1) wild oats (2) larkspur (3) helichrysum (4)

4 Starting at the left back edge of the basket, insert the bunches of wild oats, bringing them through to rest over the front right edge.

5 Cut the larkspur into short lengths and insert, following the same line.

6 Intersperse with helichrysum.

7 Fill the centre of the basket with the remaining flowers.

8 Make up a bow of dark ribbon and glue to the basket, allowing the ends to trail along the front and side.

9 Make up a bow of the paler shade of ribbon and glue it on to the darker bow.

23

Swag

A traditional garland can be displayed flat on a table, looped across the front of a table or hung on a wall. In this design a garland has been incorporated with stiffened calico to form an elegant wall hanging swag.

Materials
Piece of wire netting, 6 × 30in (15 × 75cm)
Sphagnum moss
Black stub wires; black reel wire
Quick-drying glue (or hot glue-gun)
Piece of calico 18 × 36in (45 × 90cm)
Fabric stiffening compound
White stem tape

Dried flowers
Leather fern *Arachniodes adiantiformis*
Eucalyptus blue gum *Eucalyptus saligna*
Love-in-a-mist *Nigella damascena*
Helichrysum *Helichrysum bracteatum*
Oats *Avena fatua*
Nipplewort *Lapsana communis*
Lichen *Cladonia sp.*

Preparation
1 Make a thin moss tube (refer to Better Techniques). Leave the tube to dry completely before using it.

2 Make mixed bunches of flowers, seed heads and oats and wire them together leaving 2 wire legs (refer to Better Techniques).

3 Mount foliage singly.

Working the design
4 Start by mounting leaves into one end of the moss tube, pushing the wires through then turning the ends back into the moss.

5 Now insert the bunches of flowers, seed heads and oats, surrounding each bunch with leaves. Continue along the tube until it is completely covered.

6 Cut the calico into a triangular shape, crumple it into a swag shape and spray with fabric stiffening compound. (Alternatively, brush the fabric with PVA adhesive thinly, then crumple into a swag and leave to dry.)

7 Glue the top of the swag to the stiffened calico. Bend and arrange the garland along and under the calico, removing any flowers necessary for the swag to lie flat. Secure the swag with glue and fill in any bare patches with lichen.

8 Twist four long stub wires together with a hook at one end and wire legs at the other. Bend the legs into the top end of the swag securely. Cover the hook with white stem tape.

Begin by mounting leaves into the moss tube at one end. Push the wire legs through then turn back into the moss.

Gift of grapes and flowers

Here is a delightful way to present both fruit and flowers together. Preserved statice and strawflowers are used to edge the basket and, for fragrance, small bunches of lavender sprigs and grasses decorate the basket ends.

Materials
Oval shaped basket
Quick-drying glue (or hot glue-gun)
Black reel wire

Dried flowers and grasses
Blue statice *Limonium Sinuatum*
Everlasting *Anaphalis*
Canary grass, dyed maroon *Phalaris*
Lavender *Lavandula Spica*

Preparation
1 Wire together small bunches of statice and everlastings. Trim the stems to 1in (2.5cm). Make sufficient to go round the perimeter of the basket.

2 Wire together reed grasses and stems of lavender to make 2 bunches.

Working the design
3 Spread glue along the basket edge at one end and attach one of the bunches of grasses and lavender.

4 Now continue to spread glue along the rim of the basket from this point, positioning bunches of statice and everlastings along the basket edge, so that each one covers the stems of the previous

Glue a bunch of lavender and seed heads on the basket rim then add bunches of statice and strawflowers.

bunch. Work in the same way until one side of the basket is covered.

5 Fix the second lavender and grasses bunch in place, then continue with the bunches of flowers. Finish by tucking the stems of the last bunch under the lavender.

Country gift
For a gift from the country, line a handled basket with green fabric, sticking the edge over the basket rim. Decorate the basket with yellow helichrysum and clumps of mauve statice. Fill the basket with fresh eggs.

For an Easter gift, decorate the basket rim with dried yellow and green flowers and fill the basket with real or chocolate eggs. For a housewarming gift, you might edge a basket with pink and white flowers and fill it with matching scented soaps.

6 Take individual heads of reed grass and touch the ends with glue. Insert among the flowers to break up the solidness of texture and add height.

7 Choose a tissue paper in a colour to tone with the flowers. Put it in the basket and rest the grapes on the tissue.

Heart-shaped arrangement

Although the heart shape and red roses are a traditional theme for St Valentine's day, this arrangement of dried flowers and lace could also be used as a Ruby wedding presentation gift.

Materials
Florist's foam
Heart-shaped container (such as a baking tin)
Aluminium foil
Pins
Cream-coloured lace edging, 2in (5cm) wide (see note)
Cream-coloured polyester satin ribbon. ⅛in (3mm) wide, 1yd (91cm)

Dried flowers
Red roses *Rosa*

Note: To estimate the length of lace edging required, measure round the heart-shaped container and triple the measurement.

Preparation
1 Using the container as a guide, cut the foam into a heart shape.

2 Wrap and mould the foil round the base and sides of the foam shape, leaving the top surface clear.

Working the design
3 Starting at the top of the heart, gather the lace and pin round the top edge of the foam heart, inserting the pins under the edge of the lace so that they do not show.

4 Cut the rose stems to about 1in (2.5cm) long and insert roses into the outside edge of the foam heart.

5 Use more roses to fill in the centre.

6 Wire ribbon loops (refer to Better Techniques) and tuck the wire ends into the heart at the bottom left-hand edge.

7 Wire a double ribbon bow and insert at the top right-hand edge.

Gather the lace round the heart shape and pin in place.

Special gifts
For a very special birthday or anniversary gift, cut a card template of the recipient's first name initial and use this to cut florist's dry foam to shape. Wrap the foam in foil leaving the top surface clear. Edge with lace and decorate with dried flowers.

Corsage of hyacinths

Hyacinths, with their perfectly shaped florets and fine fragrance, are ideal for breaking down and re-assembling to make a corsage. The method of wiring individual florets is called 'piping'.

Materials
Silver stub wires
Silver reel wire
White stem tape

Fresh flowers and leaves
Blue hyacinth head *Hyacinthus orientalis*
Iris leaves *Iris reticulata*
Jerusalem sage *Phlomis*

Preparation
1 Break down the hyacinth flower head into florets.

2 Starting with the buds, take each floret and insert a stub wire into the base.

3 Push 2 more stub wires into the floret, at right angles to each other. Repeat with all the florets.

4 Push a wire through the back of each of the Jerusalem sage leaves. Bend down the ends. Twist one end round the leaf stem and the other wire so that 2 wire legs are left.

5 Split the iris leaves into thin lengths. Reverse the leaf so that the underside is on top and wire into bows.

6 Bind all the wire legs with stem tape (refer to Better Techniques).

Push a stub wire through the vein on the back of the leaf. Bend the wires down and bind one round the stem.

Insert a stub wire into the bottom of the floret, then push 2 more through at right angles.

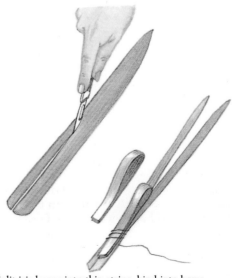

Split iris leaves into thin strips, bind into bows under side out. Assemble with strips.

Working the design

7 Starting with the buds, bind the florets and leaf bows together with stem tape. Continue binding down, adding florets and bows to build the corsage into a triangular shape.

8 To finish the corsage, trim the wire ends and bind with stem tape.

Prayer book spray
Make the corsage with a white hyacinth and white ribbons. Neaten the ends of a 12in (30cm) length of 2in (5cm)-wide piece of double-sided white satin ribbon. Pin or tape to the cover of a bride's prayer book.

Corsage of gladioli

There is a revival of the charming custom of wearing flowers, not only for weddings but for evening occasions, in the hair or on dresses.

Materials
Silver reel wire
Silver stub wires
Black stub wires
Stem tape

Fresh flowers
Gladiola *Gladiolus*
Begonia leaves *Begonia rex*
Broom *Cytisus*

Preparation
1 Choose a floret of a gladiola which is just opening and a further two at the next stage.

2 Insert a black stub wire into the base of the three florets (refer to Better Techniques).

3 Push 2 silver stub wires through the base of each floret at right angles. Bend the ends down and bind to the stub wire coming from the base.

4 Trim budding stems of broom and bind into small bunches with reel wire, leaving 2 short wire legs.

5 Place a begonia leaf in your hand, face down. Push a length of silver reel wire through the centre vein a short way up the leaf making a small stitch, leaving about 5in (12.5cm) of wire at each side.

6 Bend the ends down, bind one end round the leaf stem and then around the other wire, leaving 2 wire legs.

7 Cover all the stems with stem tape.

Bind the smallest gladiola to the two larger, prepared gladioli in a straight line.

Flowers for corsages
Freesia Wire individual florets and assemble as instructed for the hyacinth corsage.
Roses Wire rose leaves, use one tight bud, one flower just open and one full-blown rose.
Orchids For a bride's mother, wire and tape the stems of 2 cymbidium orchids and some variegated ivy. Add a ribbon bow to tone with the outfit.

Working the design

8 Take the smallest gladiola and, using reel wire, bind in the other two flowers in a straight line. Trim wire ends and bind in tightly.

9 Add broom and begonia leaves to break up the edges of the arrangement, binding them in with stem tape.

10 Finish with a bunch of broom to add length.

11 Trim the ends of the corsage to make a short handle. Bind with stem tape.

To keep a corsage fresh, place it in an airtight container on a bed of dampened and crumpled tissue paper. Surround and cover the corsage with dry tissue, snap on the container lid and keep in a cool place, or in the refrigerator set at its warmest setting.

Tussie mussie

These aromatic herb posies became popular in the 16th century when they were carried to ward off bad smells and were thought to give protection against disease.

Materials
Green stem tape
Ribbon

Fresh flowers and herbs (and their meanings)
White rose *Rosa* (Silent love)
Geranium *Pelargonium* (Comfort)
Gypsophila *Gypsophila paniculata* (Elegance)
Mint *Mentha viridis* (Wisdom)
Thyme *Thymus vulgaris* (Courage)
Sage *Salvia officinalis* (Esteem)
Fennel *Foeniculum vulgare* (Flattery)
Parsley *Petroselinum crispum* (Festivity)
Rosemary *Rosmarinus officinalis* (Remembrance)
Lavender *Lavandula officinalis* (Silence)
Bay *Laurus nobilis* (Glory)
Marjoram *Origanum Majorana* (Blushes)
Basil *Ocimum Basilicum* (Good wishes)

Bind the stems of the rose and geranium together.

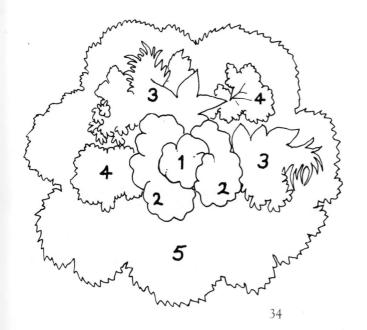

Rose (1) geranium head (2), mixed herbs (3) gypsophila (4) geranium leaves (5).

Flowers and herbs had symbolic meaning, enabling messages to be incorporated into a tussie mussie. Tussie mussies can be dried for culinary purposes by hanging upside-down (refer to Better Techniques).

Working the design

1 Position the rose in the centre of a multi-flowered stem of geranium.

2 Bind the stems together.

3 Surround the geranium with bunches of mixed herbs, interspersing with stems of gypsophila binding as you go.

4 Finish the posy by binding a circle of geranium leaves round the outside to make the effect of a 'frill'.

In Shakespeare's play *Hamlet*, Ophelia gathered herbs for a sad tussie mussie on the tragic death of her father (act 4, scene 5).

THREE

Small Thoughts

Flowers in baby shoes

A child's first steps is one of parents' happiest memories, followed perhaps by the purchase of the first pair of shoes. Use these tiny objects as a container for a dainty arrangement of flowers, as a constant reminder of the event.

Materials
Baby shoes
Florist's foam
Cling-film

Dried flowers
Zinnias *Zinnia elegans*
Gypsophila *Gypsophila paniculata*
Spray roses *Rosa*
Cornflowers *Centaurea cyanus*
Small pieces of green foliage
Mugwort buds *Artemisia Vulgaris*

Preparation
1 Line the shoes with cling-film. Fill with dry foam, cut to shape.

Cut the shoe shape from foam.

Working the designs
2 **Red arrangement:** cut the foliage into short lengths and bunch together at the back of the shoe in a fan shape.

3 Using tweezers, carefully insert the tiny roses.

Detail from the pair of baby shoes showing the dried arrangement.

4 Fill in with gypsophila to add lightness.

5 **Pink arrangement:** insert mugwort buds around the back and sides of the shoe.

6 Bed down the zinnias, leaving space in the centre.

7 Insert cornflowers in the centre, to form a posy.

8 To finish, tuck mugwort buds and zinnias in the shoe-bar spaces.

Florist's foams

Green foam To prepare green foam, fill a bucket with clean water to a greater depth than the height of the block. Put the block into the water but do not force it under the surface as this will cause air bubbles to remain inside. Leave the block to soak up water for about 10–20 minutes.

After a short first use, the foam can be re-used, if in the meantime it has been kept in a plastic bag. To re-use foam, take it out of the bag and re-soak in fresh water. If the top surface has been pitted by stems, turn it over for the new arrangement. Remember that foam must be kept wet when it is in use.

Brown, dry foam is very lightweight and must be securely fixed into the container. The container itself may need to be weighted, if it is supporting a large display.

Antique basket arrangement

This basket with an arrangement of bleached grasses against dark hydrangea heads would look superb displayed on a polished table in a sophisticated town setting.

Materials
Basket with handle
Florist's brown, dry foam
Florist's securing tape
Stub wires
Reel wire

Dried flowers
Hydrangea heads *Hydrangea macrophylla*
Bleached quaking grass *Briza*
Bleached hare's tail *Lagurus ovatus*
Bleached strawflowers *Helichrysum*

Preparation
1 Cut the dry foam to shape and fit it into the basket. Tape it to the handle.

Working the design
2 Break hydrangea into manageable florets and push into the foam.

3 Position the hare's tail grass to make an all-round shape.

4 Wire short lengths of quaking grasses into bunches. Intersperse between the hydrangea florets.

5 Wire helichrysum heads (refer to Better Techniques) and insert the wires deep into the basket throughout the arrangement.

Detail from the basket arrangement of hydrangea, strawflowers, quaking grass and hare's tail.

Trim quaking grass stems short and bunch together with wire.

40

Inkstand arrangement

The delicate colour and shape of dainty grape hyacinth flowers leaves little for the flower arranger to do – except to find a container of equal delicacy and charm. The latin name, Muscari, is derived from the musk scent of the flower.

Materials
Inkstand with twin inkpots
Green florist's foam, soaked

Fresh flowers
Polyanthus *Primula bullesiana*
Blue throatwort *Trachelium caeruleum*
Blue larkspur *Delphinium consolida*
Grape hyacinth *Muscari*
Variegated myrtle *Myrtus communis var.*

Preparation
1 Fill one of the inkpots with soaked foam so that about ½in (1cm) protrudes above the rim.

Working the design
2 Insert the myrtle to make a line from rear left to spill over the front of the inkstand.

Containers for flowers
Anything that can be made to hold water can contain fresh flowers. Some useful items that can be found around the home include teacups, jugs, boxes, miniature chests – and you could disguise jam and coffee jars.

A flower arranger also needs a good selection of vases. If you find a vase that has a good shape but an unattractive pattern or colour, or has a small amount of damage, scrub the vase clean then spray with matt paint in the colour required.

---

3 Group the polyanthus to make a focal point in the centre, having first made holes in the foam to accept the stems.

4 Insert the throatwort to follow the line of the foliage.

5 Position the larkspur to give depth.

6 Hold a bunch of muscari in your hand and surround with throatwort to make a posy. Trim the ends and place in the second inkwell. Fill with water.

Royal sprig
Myrtle signifies love and has been used in this connection for hundreds of years – the Romans used it to decorate the altar of the goddess Venus. A charming custom regarding myrtle was introduced to Britain when Prince Albert, Queen Victoria's husband-to-be, arranged for myrtle to be placed in her wedding bouquet. A sprig of this was struck and from it many bushes have grown. All subsequent royal brides have had a sprig of myrtle added to their wedding bouquets.

Arrangement with a candlestick

This simple arrangement is ideal for a small dinner party table, where a single candle is required. The design was inspired by the shallow, floating flower arrangements, so beloved by Victorian hostesses for their party tables.

Materials
White china flan dish
China candle stick
Florist's green foam, soaked
Florist's securing tape
Wire netting

Fresh flowers
Carnations *Dianthus caryophyllus*
Euphorbia foliage *Euphorbia marginata*
Polyanthus *Primula Polyanthus*

Preparation
1 Cut the soaked foam to the shape of the candlestick base and to the depth of the flan dish.

2 Secure the foam to the centre of the dish with florist's securing tape.

3 Surround the foam with crumpled wire netting and position the candlestick on top of the foam.

4 Half fill the dish with water.

Working the design
5 Cut the carnation stems short and position the heads round the edge of the dish.

6 Place the heads of euphorbia between the carnations.

Cut the foam to the shape of the candlestick base.
Secure the base to the centre of the flan dish.

7 Arrange the polyanthus in the centre round the base of the candlestick.

Here are some seasonal ideas for this arrangement:
Spring: Violets and primroses
Summer: Garden roses and gypsophila
Autumn: Pompom dahlias in different colours
Winter: Evergreen foliage and red berries

Garden flowers in a jug

A traditional terracotta jug blends perfectly with the old-fashioned garden flower, michaelmas daisies and the warmth of its colour tones in with the hues of the chrysanthemums.

Materials
Small terracotta jug
Green florist's foam, soaked

Fresh flowers
Michaelmas daisy *Aster novi-belgii*
Spray chrysanthemum
    Chrysanthemum-hybrid
Black, spiky leaves of *Ophiopogom planiscapus nigrescens*

Preparation
1 Cut the soaked foam block so that it fits into the jug and about ½in (1cm) stands above the rim. (Refer to Better Techniques.)

Cut foam should be soaked for at least 15 minutes before using it. If the vase you are using is tall, make sure your arrangement conceals the foam.

Michaelmas daisy sprays (1) spray chrysanthemums (2), ophiogom leaves (3).

Working the design

2 Break the michaelmas daisies into small sprays and insert into the foam.

3 Fill out the arrangement by inserting the spray chrysanthemums.

4 Add the *ophiopogom* leaves to break up the solidness of the shape.

OPHIOPOGOM is a most unusual plant in being one of the few nearly black-leaved plants in existence. In cultivation, the plant requires a sunny or part-shaded position. It is a slow creeper, producing the striking foliage which is so important to flower arrangers.

Arrangement in a tureen

An old, small tureen serves as an excellent container for this small arrangement in pink and silver. The design is in the classic triangular shape that is just as beautiful when viewed from the side as from above.

Materials
Small tureen or serving dish
Florist's green foam, soaked

Fresh flowers
Silver mound *Artemisia schmidtiana nana*
Silver-toned cyclamen leaves *Cyclamen persicum*
Pink broom *Cytisus praecox*
Pink roses *Rosa*
Pink spray carnations *Dianthus caryophyllus*
Bouvardia *Bouvardia hybrid*

Preparation
1 Pack the soaked florist's foam into the tureen and cut off 1in (2.5cm) above the top.

Working the design
2 Starting in the middle, insert mixed foliage to create the outline.

3 Insert the roses, starting from the back and working through to the centre.

4 Break up the spray carnations and insert the flowers, bringing the line through from left to right.

5 Fill in throughout the display with groups of broom.

6 Add the bouvardia to fall over the front edge of the tureen.

7 Finish with a ring of cyclamen leaves to highlight the roses and soften the front edge of the tureen.

Use cyclamen leaves to soften the front edge of the arrangement.

These small tureens were, in fact, containers for sauce, made in the shape of the main vegetable dishes instead of the more usual 'boat' shapes. They can sometimes be found in antique shops, having lost their ladle and lid.

FOUR

Festive Flowers

Easter arrangement

This classic fan shape is now considered rather stiff as a design but there are still occasions and venues when this type of formal display is required as an integral part of the background.

Materials
Vase
Florist's green foam, soaked
Wire netting

Fresh flowers
Boston fern *Nephrolepis exaltate*
Mimosa *Acacia dealbata hybrid*
Tulips *Tulipa*
Narcissus Soleil d'Or *Narcissus*
Lilies *Lilium hybrid*

Preparation
1 Cut a piece of soaked foam to fit into the vase and cut off the top about 1in (2.5cm) above the rim.

2 Cover the foam with wire netting, crumpling the wire round the neck of the vase to hold it in place.

Mimosa (1), foliage (2) lily spray (3) open lilies (4), tulips (5) narcissus and mimosa (6).

Working the design

3 Create a basic symmetrical fan outline with foliage and mimosa.

4 Insert more foliage and mimosa from the front, sweeping out and down to lie over the front of the vase.

5 Position the first spray of lilies at the centre back to define the height.

6 Insert the other lilies to form a curve, passing through the centre and finishing with a curving left 'arm'.

7 Position the tulips to spill gracefully over the front of the vase.

8 Fill in where required with narcissus and mimosa.

Hallowe'en basket

Decorations for Hallowe'en are usually dressed in black and orange – and at this time of year, Chinese lantern seed heads are at their best in the garden. This rustic wall decoration is arranged in a special wall basket.

Materials
Wall basket
Florist's foam
Black stub wires
Black reel wire

Dried flowers
Large poppy seed heads *Papaver orientalis*
Chinese lantern seed heads
    Physalis franchetii
Mixed grasses, dyed black

Preparation
1 Fill the basket with dried foam. Cut to a convex shape.

Working the design
2 Insert the dyed grasses in a semi-circular shape along the back and front edges of the basket.

3 Insert a stub wire into the base of each Chinese lantern (refer to Better Techniques) and glue to secure.

Detail of the basket showing Chinese lantern heads trailing over the front.

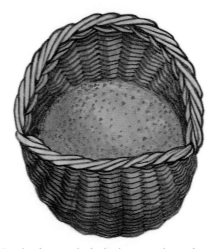

Cut dry foam to fit the basket, trim the surface to a convex shape.

4 Insert Chinese lanterns in a semi-circular row at the back of the basket, in front of the grasses.

5 Insert a row of poppy seed heads in the very front of the basket.

6 Wire small bunches of grasses (refer to Better Techniques).

7 Fill in the centre space with Chinese lantern heads, poppy seed heads and the bunches of dyed grass.

8 Glue some Chinese lantern heads to the front of the basket to give a trailing effect.

Christmas arrangement

Although blue and silver is not generally regarded as a traditional Christmas colour scheme, the cool shades of this spectacular display have a seasonal beauty of their own. This arrangement can be used for a table or on a window sill.

Materials
Brown florist's foam
Cake stand, cork placemat or piece of
  wood
Florist's securing tape
Plastic candle holders
Black stub wires
Black reel wire
Silver spray paint
5 blue candles, 12in (30cm) long

Flowers and foliage
Dried delphinium *Delphinium consolida*
Eucalyptus *Eucalyptus cinera*
Blue conifer *Juniperus – Blue carpet*
Twisted willow *Salix tortuosa*
Assorted fir cones

Preparation
1 Wire all the fir cones (refer to Better
Techniques). Push these and the twisted
willow into a complete block of foam.
Put everything into a large box.

2 Spray all the items in the box with
silver paint (refer to Better Techniques).

3 Remove the cones and willow.

4 Cut the silvered foam into steps, with
the highest point at the right, to take the
candle holders (refer to the picture).

5 Fix the foam block to the base with
tape.

Working the design
6 Insert the candle holders in the block.
Put in the candles.

7 Position the conifer sprays into the
base to give shape.

8 Place a stem of delphinium at the front
left and carry the line of delphiniums to
break through the candles.

9 Insert the wired cones to provide a
focal point at the base of the candles.

10 Intersperse the arrangement with
eucalyptus sprays to give height.

11 Position the twisted willow to provide
extra interest (see picture).

Take care
Arrangements with candles in them
should not be left unattended,
particularly when dried material has
been used. Watch burning candles
carefully and extinguish and replace
them when they burn down to about
3in (7.5cm) from the arrangement.

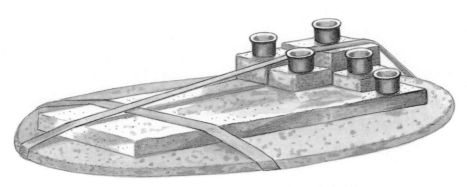

Cut the silvered foam into steps to take the candle holders.

Christmas cones

For many people, the most enjoyable part of Christmas preparations is that of dressing the tree. These pretty cones are simple to make and you can vary the colour scheme of the flowers and ribbons to suit your holiday décor.

Materials
Quick-drying glue (or a glue-gun)
Gold spray paint
Gold gift ribbon
Gold-edged, red grosgrain ribbon, ½in
    (12mm) wide

Dried flowers and grasses
Fir cones
Red cluster-flowered strawflowers
    Helichrysum italicum
Canary grass *Phalaris*
Selection of other dried grasses

Preparation
1 Clean the cones and leave in a warm
place to open.

2 Place some cones and grasses inside a
large cardboard box and spray them gold
(refer to Better Techniques).

3 Stand a gold-painted cone in the lid of
the spray can (to hold it in position) and
apply some glue to the top.

4 Arrange two 4in (10cm)-long pieces of
gold gift ribbon at right angles on the
glue. Leave to dry.

Tartan cones
This is just one of the variations that
can be worked with the basic
technique.

Do not spray the cones – leave
them in their natural state. Cut 2
pieces of ½in (12mm)-wide taffeta
tartan ribbon and glue to the top of
the cone at right angles. When dry,
cut 8in (20cm) lengths of 1in (2.5cm)-
wide tartan ribbon and glue loops to
the tops of the cones. Decorate with
red flowers, small larch cones and
natural grasses.

Tartan cones look particularly
effective if large bows of wide,
matching tartan ribbon are tied to
the Christmas tree branches.

5 Cut an 8in (20cm) length of gold-edged
grosgrain ribbon and fold to make a
loop. Glue to the cone with 1in (2.5cm)
ends protruding each side.

6 Glue pieces of grasses and strawflowers
to cluster round the cone on top of gold
ribbon.

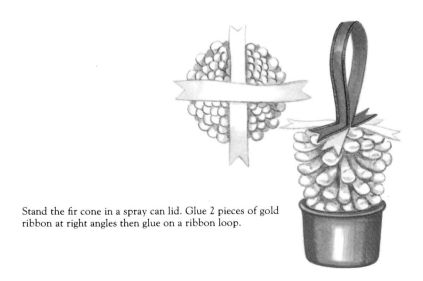

Stand the fir cone in a spray can lid. Glue 2 pieces of gold
ribbon at right angles then glue on a ribbon loop.

Door wreath

This golden-toned arrangement is just the thing for the door to welcome guests to a 50th wedding anniversary party. This is an opportunity to use any faded, dried flowers you may have by spraying them gold.

Materials
14in (36cm) diameter florist's foam ring
   (or a moss-covered wreath)
Black stub wires
Black reel wire
Gold spray paint
2yd (1.8m) of glossy, wire-edged ribbon,
   3in (7.5cm) wide

Dried material
Poppy seed heads *Papaver Orientalis*
Fir cones
Dried fungus
Dried flower heads
Sea lavender *Limonium*

Preparation
1 With reel wire, make several turns round the top of the ring over a small box. Remove the box and twist the wires to make a strong loop for hanging.

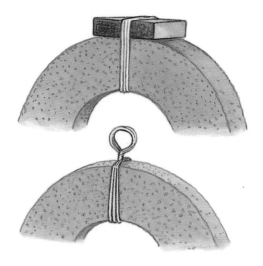

Wind reel wire round the ring and a box several times. Twist the loop to make a hanger.

2 Put all the dried material inside a large box and spray two or three times with gold paint, turning between coats and allowing the material to dry between each spraying.

Working the design
3 Insert a mixture of the gold material round the inside edge of the wreath.

4 Insert the same mixture round the outside edge of the wreath.

5 Cut the wire-edged ribbon into 6in (15cm) lengths. Make 12 wired loops (refer to Better Techniques).

6 Insert 7 of the loops at the centre top of the wreath over the position of the hanger, to make a showy bow.

7 Insert the remaining ribbon loops at regular intervals round the wreath.

8 Fill in with the remaining gold-sprayed material, taking care that a rounded and even shape is achieved.

> For a 25th anniversary, spray the dried material silver and use blue and white ribbons.

Peach and coral

It is the hidden foundation – a tilted back pyramid – that gives this dried arrangement the impression of depth. The flowers and foliage, in tones from pale peach to coral, cascade like a waterfall, and make a dramatic impact when viewed from above.

Materials
A base (such as a wicker mat)
Large block of green florist's foam
Plastic pin holders
Adhesive clay tape
Wire netting
Black stub wires
Black reel wire
Quick-drying glue (or hot glue-gun)

Dried flowers and foliage
Helichrysum *Helichrysum bracteatum*
Copper beech *Fagus sylvatica purpurea*
Gypsophila *Gypsophila paniculata*
Protea *Protea cynaroides*
Dudinea seed heads *Dudinea*
Larch cones *Larix sp.*
Reed canary grass *Phalaris arundinacea*
Poppy seed heads *Papaver orientalis*
Various kinds of dried fungi

Preparation
1 Cut a square-based pyramid, but tilted back, from dry foam.

2 Secure to the base with plastic pin holders and clay tape.

3 Cover the foam with wire netting.

4 Wire gypsophila, reed grass and dudinea seed heads into small bunches, leaving 2 wire legs (refer to Better Techniques).

Working the design
5 Insert the beech to form the outline. Position the open protea blooms in the centre.

Detail of the tilted pyramid arrangement.

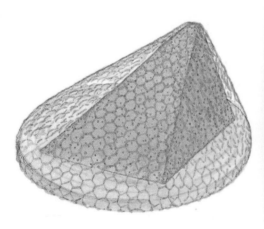

Cover the secured pyramid shape with wire netting.

6 Wire the fungus and the cones (refer to Better Techniques) and insert them in prominent positions.

7 Fill in with helichrysum, protea buds and the remaining bunches to complete the shape.

Hostess bunch

Hand-tied bunches of flowers are back in fashion and they are the perfect gift, giving lasting pleasure. This arrangement is built up in the hand, with no florist's mechanics involved. It can hang on a wall or simply rest on a dresser.

Materials
Garden string
3yd (2.7m) of 3in (7.5cm)-wide scrim
  ribbon (or paper ribbon)

Dried flowers and foliage
Blue larkspur *Delphinium consolida*
Yarrow, dyed red *Achillea filipendulina*
Artemisia foliage, dyed green *Artemisia*
Red roses *Rosa*

Working the design
1 Begin with stems of artemisia foliage to build up the basic foundation, holding the stems between thumb and forefinger. Keep the same grip all the time you are making the bunch.

2 Knot a loop of string round the stems and bind in securely.

3 Work in stems of achillea round the centre stems, then angle some more to create depth and width. Tie in.

4 Keeping the fingers in the same position, but slackening them slightly, tie in stems of larkspur.

5 Gradually fill in gaps by inserting roses and the remaining artemisia foliage.

6 Fasten the string ends in a knot, leaving a loop at the back of the bunch.

7 Finish by tying scrim ribbon round the bunch and tie a large bow.

Dyeing flowers
Almost any pale-coloured flowers can be dyed using food colouring. Mix 2 teaspooons of colouring with 1¼ cups of hot water into a jar. Stand the jar in a bucket. Strip the foliage from the stems, split the ends and stand the flowers in the solution. Allow the flowers to drink until the colour is up to the tips. You may need to experiment with the quantity of food colouring to get the desired shade. Grasses can also be dyed in this way. Flowers can be dried after dyeing.

FIVE

Mostly Foliage

Foliage pedestal

A mixed, fresh foliage arrangement can last for many weeks and is a constant delight. This arrangement makes good use of the stiffness of some of its component branches and is designed to lighten a dark corner in a room.

Materials
Pedestal container
Adhesive clay tape
Plastic pin holders
Green florist's foam, soaked
Florist's tape

Fresh foliage
Jerusalem sage *Phlomis*
Silver mound *Artemesia schmidtiana nana*
Elaeagnus *Elaeagnus angustifolia*
Sedum *Sedum roseum*
Begonia leaves *Begonia rex*

When making a mixed green foliage display always remember to sponge all leaves clean before starting the arrangement. For an extra shine, wipe over the leaves with cotton wool soaked in mayonnaise.

Preparation
1 Fix the soaked foam block to the pedestal dish with plastic pin holders and clay tape. Secure firmly with florist's tape.

Working the design
2 Prune the branches of elaeagnus to shape them and insert them into the foam to make the upper and lower shapes.

3 Following this line, insert the other foliage to balance the shape.

4 Fill in the centre, making a focal point of the begonia leaves with some of the sedum.

5 Top up the dish with water at frequent intervals.

Fix the soaked foam block in the pedestal dish. Insert the evergreen branches to make the upper and lower shapes.

Christmas garland

*Fresh foliage garlands shrivel quickly in warm rooms
but florists can provide artificial garlands that look almost real
and last from year to year.*

Materials
Artificial fir garland
Black stub wires
Black reel wire
6yd (5.50m) of crushed, red paper ribbon

Dried material
Fir cones
Fir tree bark
Nuts, nut cases
Lichens or moss

Preparation
1 Wire all the cones, nuts and nut cases
and make bundles of the bark (refer to
Better Techniques).

2 Divide the lichen and mount into
bunches.

3 Decide on the position of the finished
garland and offer it up. Mark the position
of the fixing points and wire in loops of
binding wire at these places.

Working the design
4 Spread out the garland and distribute
the wired decorations evenly along its
length. Secure them to the garland by
twisting the two mounting wires around
the garland.

5 Trim off the surplus wire and fold back
the ends to prevent them from scratching
your hands or furnishings.

6 Tie a large bow for the centre and 2
smaller ones for the corners. Wire them
on.

7 Divide the remaining ribbon lengthways into 2 narrow widths. Keep back 2 pieces for the garland ends. Make small bows with the rest and distribute them along the garland.

On Christmas morning, wire small red apples, clementines and bunches of cinnamon sticks and add them to the garland for extra colour.

8 Hang the garland in position and tie ribbons around the hanging ends.

Winter bride's bouquet

*This glorious bouquet would warm the heart of any
winter bride. The rich, vibrant tones of the mixed foliage require
the addition of the minimum of flowers.*

Materials
Black stub wires
Black reel wire
Stem tape or gutta percha
Satin ribbon

Fresh flowers and foliage
Berginia leaves *Berginia Bressingham ruby*
Cotoneaster horizontalis
Leucothoe fontanesiana
Skimmia japonica rubella
Chamaecyparis thyoides ericoides
5 deep red roses *Rosa*

Preparation
1 Start by grouping the foliage on a
table, in a rough pear shape.

2 Strip 4-6in (10-15cm) of foliage from
the end of each stem. If there are some
stems that are too short for this
treatment, mount them on 22 gauge wire
and cover them with stem tape (refer to
Better Techniques).

Working the design
3 Begin to arrange the bouquet in your
hand, building a foundation of *Berginia
Bressingham ruby* leaves. Tie the bunch
with reel wire.

4 Gradually work round the outside of
the central core of foliage by adding the
mixed foliages, positioning them at
angles, passing each stem between your
forefinger and thumb and securely
binding in some of the stems so that they
appear to cascade out of the bunch.

5 Loosen your grip on the bunch as you
bed the roses into the centre.

It is an advantage to have a large
mirror in front of you when you are
making a bride's bouquet so that you
can constantly check its shape from
the front and the sides. As the bride
walks to the altar, it is the side view
of the bouquet which is viewed
mostly.

6 Break up the solidness by positioning
small leaves and buds of the various
foliages, binding in each stem.

7 Place the last remaining stems of
foliage, letting the *cotoneaster* trail.

All the foliages in this loose bouquet
have been carefully selected as
examples to grow and give year-
round colour to a garden and thus,
most useful to a flower arranger.
Berginia Bressingham ruby is a
robust grower, making a compact
clump of glossy, green leaves which
turn to a burnished maroon with a
crimson underside in winter. In the
spring, it produces bold spikes of
deep rose-coloured flowers.
Cotoneaster is a deciduous shrub,
indispensable in the garden for
ground cover, screens and hedges
against walls, with an abundance of
berries in autumn and winter.
Chamaecyparis *thyoides ericoides*
is a slow-growing conifer that can be
grown as a container plant. It has
maroon leaves that provide a good
show in summer and will continue
in a normal winter.

8 Hold the bouquet in your fingertips while pulling up each wired stem. Bend these round the bound section, tucking the ends of the wires into the stems.

9 Bind tightly and cut the wires.

10 Now trim and shape the natural stems.

11 Cover the binding with ribbon and add a tied bow.

75

Bridesmaid's headdress

In recent years, there has been a revival of interest in fresh flower headdresses. They can be made to any size from a small coronet to be worn on top of the head to a full circlet, worn on the forehead. Here is a quick method for making a circlet.

Materials
Black reel wire
White stem tape
White satin ribbon

Fresh flowers
Flowering jasmine *Jasminum polyanthum*

Preparation
1 Choose a jasmine plant that has plenty of growth and is just coming into flower. The jasmine will probably have been trained on a wire so lift the ends out of the pot.

2 Cut the stem or stems at the base and stretch out the plant and its wire on the table.

Bend the foliage and wire into a circle, push the foliage to one end and start to tape the wire. Then move the foliage and tape the remaining wire.

76

Working the design

3 Pushing the foliage towards the centre, bend the plant and wire into a circle. Measure the head and add 1in (2.5cm). Cut the wire to this measurement.

4 Slide the foliage back and forth while you cover the wire with stem tape.

5 Bend the ends of the wire to make a hook and eye, so that the headdress can be fastened round the head.

6 Space the foliage evenly around and trim where necessary. Tie a bow with long streamers and wire it to the back of the circlet.

Chrysanthemums in a glass

Green and blue – and water – suggest coolness and tranquillity.
This deceptively simple arrangement has a purity of line that
enables it to fit into modern as well as traditional surroundings.

Materials
Green sundae glass
Florist's blue glass nuggets

Fresh flowers
Yellow spider chrysanthemums
  Chrysanthemum indicum hybrid
Leaves of spider plant *Chlorophytum*
  comosum variegatum

Preparation
1 Fill the sundae glass three-quarters full
with blue glass nuggets.

Working the design
2 Choose some longer leaves from the
spider plant and insert them deep into
the glass nuggets on the left hand side,
leaning to the left.

3 Select shorter leaves and insert them at
the centre back of the glass.

4 Feed in some of the smallest leaves at
the right. (Do not use more than a few
leaves at each point.)

5 Select one perfect yellow spider
chrysanthemum and position it at centre
front.

6 Take 2 half-open chrysanthemum buds
on slightly longer stems and place one to
the the left and the other behind the
main flower.

7 Add a few more glass nuggets if
required and·fill the sundae glass with
water.

This classic arrangement can also be
made using the small sea shells or
little pebbles that you have so
carefully collected at the seashore.
These often look very dull when
brought home but when re-immersed
in water they glisten again.

Ideas for arrangements with glass
● Cram tulips into a glass tank to see
their full beauty.
● Float camellias in water in a glass
cakestand.
● Half-fill a sundae glass with water.
Trim the stem of a full-blown rose
and put into the glass. On a round
table, set one before each guest.
● Fill small whisky tumblers with
purple glass nuggets. Fill the glasses
with water, insert 3 large marigolds
in each. Arrange the glasses down the
centre of a long dining table.
● Set a single flower head in each of
a collection of cut-glass ashtrays.
Carefully tone the flower colours so
that a harmonious effect is achieved.
● For a table centre, balance glass
containers – cake stands, stemmed
champagne glasses and sundae dishes
– one on another to make a balanced
shape. Fill the containers with water,
position flower heads and trailing
foliages to form a cascade.

SIX

Something
Different

Driftwood arrangement

The art of Japanese flower arranging known as Ikebana dates back to the 6th century. It takes years of study to perfect the art of Ikebana but this arrangement, in the style of Moribana form – an upright style – will encourage you in the study of texture, shape and form.

Materials
Pieces of driftwood
Needlepoint pin holder
Container (small dish or plastic food tub)

Fresh flowers and plants
Blue iris *Iris hollandica hybrid*
Twisted willow *Salix tortuosa*

> If you do not have driftwood, set up the arrangement as follows: set a pin holder off centre in a shallow dish. Place the iris and willow and then cover the pinholder with carefully-chosen small pebbles and rocks.

Preparation
1 Place the pin holder in the chosen container. Fill the container with water.

2 Arrange the driftwood to make an attractive shape and so that it conceals the container.

Working the design
3 Position the iris (study the picture). The art is to make the flowers appear to be growing straight from earth towards the sun.

4 Select a piece of twisted willow and place to harmonize.

Ikebana
Fourteen hundred years ago, the arranging of flowers in harmony with the Buddhist temples was considered to be a sacred rite. Later, schools of flower arranging were founded, headed by masters who created rigid forms of symbolism. Throughout the centuries the study of Ikebana has been part of Japanese culture. Students learn that the positioning of the flowers has deep religous and philosophical significance which harmonizes with aesthetic feeling. The first 3 principal stems that are positioned are known as Heaven, Earth and Man.

Ikebana International was formed in 1958 to stimulate the study and spread of the art and there are now more than 200 Chapters in the world. Their motto is 'Friendship through flowers'.

> The beautiful variety of iris used in this arrangement is called 'Wedgwood' and was developed in the United States of America. The flower enjoys world-wide popularity as an all-year-round floristry flower.

Roses and freesias

*The unusual combination of peach and mauve flowers
set into a letter rack effectively draws attention to and enhances
the natural warmth of the wood colour. This shows how a dark
corner or a wood-panelled room can be lightened with
a subtle colour scheme.*

Materials
Wooden letter rack
Cling-film
Florist's green foam, soaked

Fresh flowers and foliage
Peach roses *Rosa*
Mauve freesias *Freesia hybrid*
Ajuga foliage *Ajuga reptens*

Preparation
1 Line the letter rack with cling-film.

2 Pack the letter rack with soaked
florist's foam and cut off about
1in (2.5cm) above the front edge.

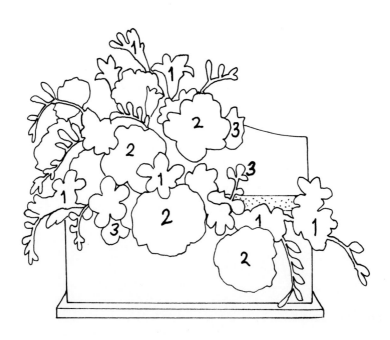

Freesias (1) roses (2) ajuga foliage (3).

Working the design
3 Position and insert the freesias to give
the required height and shape, allowing
them to sweep over to the right.

4 Now insert the roses, following the
same line as the freesias. Place several to
create depth.

5 Cover the exposed foam by inserting
ajuga leaves.

85

Hellebores and cyclamen

Dusky mauve hellebores and alpine cyclamen are treasures for flower arrangers who may be searching the garden for material in the winter months. The simplicity of these flowers when used with ivy draws the eye to the detail of the box they are set into.

Materials
Small wooden box with a hinged lid
Cling-film
Florist's green foam, soaked

Fresh flowers and foliage
Lenten roses *Helleborus orientalis*
Alpine cyclamen *Cyclamen coum*
Alstroemeria *Alstroemeria aurantiaca*
Ivy *Hedera helix*

Cut the foam higher at the back of the box so that it supports the lid open.

Flower arrangers are grateful for the hellebores in January and February when their flowers provide a touch of colour in the garden. *Helleborus niger* is the true Christmas rose (which rarely lives up to its name), and is creamy-white. *Helleborus orientalis* is the Lenten rose with hybrids from white to deep pink and plum-purple. *Helleborus foetidus* has greenish flowers while *corsicus* flowers are green-white.

Preparation

1 Carefully line the box with cling-film.

2 Pack soaked foam into the box and cut off about 1in (2.5cm) above the front rim, sloping up towards the back so that the hinged lid is supported part open.

3 Condition the lenten roses (refer to Better Techniques). Insert them into the box in small clusters.

4 Arrange the alstroemeria florets to spill over the edge of the box.

5 Group the cyclamen to lie over the lid.

6 Balance the design with ivy.

Arrangement in a teapot

Many people have small teapots that they have either collected for their prettiness, or which have been discarded because they have lost their lids. This Chinese teapot is a treasured keepsake and makes a charming table centre when filled with spring flowers.

Materials
Teapot
Wire netting

Fresh flowers and plants
White daffodils *Narcissus pseudonarcissus*
Polyanthus *Primula polyanthus*
Maidenhair fern *Adiantum*
Blue anemone *Anemone coronia*

Preparation
1 Crumple up the wire netting and push it into the teapot. Fill the pot with water.

Working the design
2 Use fern and polyanthus leaves to cover the edge of the pot.

3 Position the anemone in the centre.

4 Insert daffodils and polyanthus flowers to form a casual posy round the anemone.

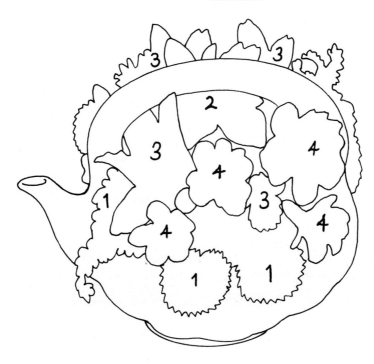

Fern and polyanthus leaves (1) anemone (2) daffodils (3) polyanthus flowers (4).

88

Foliage for arrangements

Foliages are almost indispensable in flower arranging and their shape and colour can determine the final display. There are several kinds that the flower arranger will find useful.

Angelica *Archangelica officinalis* The leaves are a good, lime green.

Dogwood *Cornus alba* has striped green and white leaves.

Decorative kale and cabbage have green, white and red foliage.

Elaeagnus pungens are lime, green and yellow in winter.

Hostas have many varieties that provide leaves in a range of colours from yellow to green and striped grey-green.

Pieris Formosa is a shrub with greenish-white 'lily of the valley'-shaped flowers which are useful for cascading arrangements.

Grey foliages in a flower arranger's garden these should include *artemisia arborescens, eryngium planum, eucalyptus gunnii*, and *ruta graveolens*.

Polyanthus and pussy willow

During the Second World War, it became difficult to obtain palm fronds for Palm Sunday arrangements and pussy willow was often used instead. Now the handsome stems with their velvety buds are often chosen for Easter arrangements in their own right.

Materials
Large basket
Plastic sheeting
Broken flowerpot pieces
Potting compost
Glass jar
Wire netting

Fresh flowers and foliage
Polyanthus plants *Primula polyanthus*
Pussy willow *Salix purpurea*

Preparation
1 Line the basket with plastic sheeting and trim off the excess.

2 Place some broken pieces of flowerpot in the basket to aid drainage.

3 Put some of the potting compost in the basket.

Working the design
4 Plant the polyanthus round the edge.

5 Crumple the wire netting and push it into the glass jar.

6 Push the jar into the centre of the basket. Keep the lid on while you fill up any spaces in the basket with potting compost.

7 Remove the jar lid. Arrange the palm, cutting the stems to varying heights and splaying them out to form an all-round shape.

8 Fill the jar with water and, from time to time, keep it, and the whole basket, topped up.

Detail of the Easter arrangement of polyanthus and pussy willow.

90

Flowers with vegetables

Some of the most interesting shapes in the garden are in the vegetable patch. Mixed with dried material, a stunning display can be quickly achieved. In this arrangement, shades of brown and orange lead into a main sweep of deep red tones.

Materials

Heavy, earthenware bowl
Brown florist's foam
Stub wires
Wire netting
Garden canes
Terracotta flowerpots

Dried flowers

Hydrangea heads *Hydrangea macrophylla*
Copper beech *Fagus sylvatica purpurea*
Black-eared barley *Hordeum sp.*
Lotus seed heads *Nelumbo lucifera*
Sweet corn *Zea maize*
Various kinds of dried fungus, gourds
Lichen, dyed maroon *Cladonia*
Globe artichoke flower *Cynara scolymus*
Variety of vegetables

Preparation

1 Fill the bowl with foam, cover with wire netting and wrap the netting over so that it grips the sides of the bowl.

2 Push short garden canes into the bottoms of the heavier vegetables. Push strong stub wires into the lighter ones to make mounting points.

3 Bunch and wire stems of barley using the two-leg method (see Better Techniques).

Working the design

4 Insert beech and corn cobs to shape and give height to the arrangement.

5 Lay some beech, gourds and fungus at the base of the bowl to give width on the right.

6 Fill the centre of the arrangement with mounted mushrooms, onions, lotus seed heads and gourds.

7 Now begin the main sweep. Lay the lichen to make a sweep down and forward on the left side.

8 Lay one flowerpot on its side to the left of the bowl and cover the pot by inserting parsnips and sweet corn.

9 Tuck the artichoke flower into the flowerpot and fill with hydrangea.

10 Lay the second pot in front and tip in an aubergine. Position chillies and a red onion to spill out of this pot.

11 Use the remaining chillies and red onions to fill all the gaps.

12 Fill in the outline with hydrangea and lichen.

94

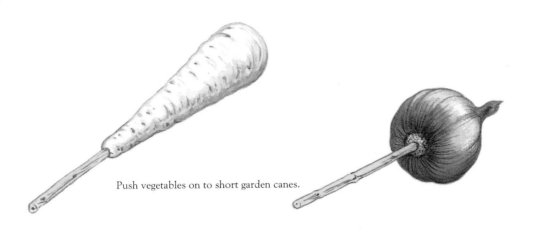

Push vegetables on to short garden canes.

Better Techniques

Even if you are arranging flowers just for your home, an investment into basic equipment will save you compromises that, in the long term, could spoil your enjoyment of the craft. Some professional tips and advice are also in this chapter.

TOOLS AND EQUIPMENT

Scissors

Florist's scissors are strong and intended for heavy work. They will cut through hard stems, and wire.

Lightweight florist's scissors are light in the hand and sharp. Use them for cutting stems and ribbon.

Wire cutters are a useful extra and will help you to preserve your florist's scissors.

Stem strippers are useful for clearing stems of thorns and foliage.

Plastic pin holders

These are embedded into foam blocks which are then fastened into containers with clay tape.

Handling wire netting

Measure a length twice the diameter of the container and cut it with florist's scissors. Crumple the wire netting evenly to fit into the container. Use the points of a pair of scissors to lift the mesh to make even spaces. Secure the netting to the container by tying it with string, fixing it with reel wire or by securing it in place with securing tape.

Wires

Stub wires

These are used to make false stems for preserved and artificial flowers and leaves They can also be inserted into hollow stems and can be usecd to strengthen limp stems. The most useful sizes are 22g, 7in (18cm) long and 20g, 12in (30cm) long.

Size	Thickness in mm	Standard wire gauge no.
Heavy	1.25	18
	1.00	19
	0.90	20
Medium	0.71	22
	0.56	24
Fine	0.46	26
	0.38	28
Very fine	0.32	30
	0.28	32
	0.24	34
	0.20	36

Silver wires are for corsage and bouquet work. 28g is the most useful size and is available on a reel.

Reel wire is a fine, strong wire, sold on a reel and is used for bunching and binding. 'Blue annealed' wire has a black look.

Other equipment
Tapes
Adhesive clay tape comes in a roll protected with a paper backing. It sticks firmly to glass and china and can be removed without damaging the surface.

Securing tape is semi-waterproof and is used to secure foam or wire netting to a container or base. It comes in two widths ¼in and ½in wide (6mm and 12mm).

Stem tape and gutta percha are both tapes for covering wire. Gutta percha comes from a natural tree gum while stem tape is man-made. Stem tape comes in pale and dark green, brown and white.

FLORIST'S MECHANICS
This term is used for anything which holds or supports flowers in an arrangement.

Staysoft
This is a trade name for a type of 'modelling clay' used to hold a small display of dried material.

Candle spikes
These fix into foam block and hold candles securely.

Wire netting Sometimes referred to as chicken wire, this is one of the most useful of florist's mechanics. It comes in various mesh sizes but 2in (5cm) is best as it crumples easily and can be moulded without becoming too rigid.

Florist's foam
Green foam is sold in blocks and is for fresh flower arranging. It should be well-soaked before use.

Brown, dry foam is for dried arrangements and is available in cylinders, cones, balls, ovals etc as well as in blocks.

   Both types of foam are easily cut to shape with a sharp knife. Green foam can be shaped before soaking or afterwards but it is preferable to shape it when dry.

Buying fresh flowers
When buying flowers, buy from a reputable florist who will have thoroughly conditioned the flowers before sale. Look for general freshness: There should be no obvious signs of disease or wilting and the stems should feel firm and the leaves crisp. The ends of the stems should not appear slimy when lifted from the water.

   If you are buying flowers from a street trader, take note that the flowers have been protected from wind and sun by an awning.

   When buying particular types of flowers there are other specific points to note.

Tight buds In flowers such as daffodils, tulips, pinks etc, the buds must show some signs of colour otherwise they may not open.

Multi-flower heads such as delphinium, gladiola, freesias etc. The lowest flower on the stem should be just opening. Do not buy if there are signs that the lowest floret has been removed.

Daisy-centred flowers such as daisies, spray chrysanthemums, single dahlias etc. The yellow centre must be firm with no sign of pollen being released.

FLOWER ARRANGERS' TECHNIQUES

Mounting wires

Attaching wires to flowers enables them to be secured to a base. Bind the wire round the stem leaving two 3in (7.5cm) 'legs'.

Lightweight flowers which are to be inserted into foam can be wired with reel wire. Plant material which is to be mounted into moss bases requires black stub wire with one (or two) legs.

Bind one end of the wire round the stem and the wire to make 2 legs.

False stems

To make a false stem, cut the existing flower stem to 1in (2.5cm) below the calyx. Push a 12in (30cm) No.22 gauge wire through the calyx, extending about 1in (2.5cm) on the other side. Bend down the wire ends, pinching one against the calyx and leaving the other as a single wire 'leg', Cover the calyx and leg with stem tape.

Ways with foliage

These can add a touch of celebration to a flower gift. The iridescent, silver colour of the reverse side of iris leaves is particularly beautiful in a silver container. Use the whole leaf and split into strips. Fold down the tip of a strip, under side out, and mount with a single wire leg. Push the leg well down into the damp foam so that the foliage can take up moisture. Gladiola foliage can be used in the same way.

Gutta-ing

This technique is used to conceal the wire of a false stem. Place the end of gutta percha (or stem tape) behind the flower calyx at a 45° angle. Tuck in the end and then twist the wired stem in the fingers while holding the tape taut. Continue twisting and taping, allowing the tape to creep down and cover the wire.

Twist the stem, allowing the tape to creep down and cover the wire.

Mounting cones

Push one end of a 12in (30cm)-long No. 20 wire between the lowest seeds of the cone leaving about 1½in (4cm) of the short end protruding. Tightly wind the wire around and through the cone seeds to meet the short end. Twist the ends together to secure. Trim the short ends flush then bend the wire under the base. Use stem tape to conceal the wire.

Push the wire between the cone seeds.

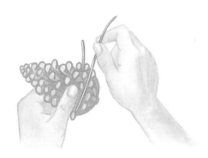

Wind the long end round, between the seeds, twist the ends together.

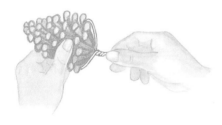

Trim the wire ends level, bend the ends under the base and cover with stem tape.

Pinning

This term is used when attaching stemless plant material to a moss or foam base with wire pins. Cut black stub wires into 3½in (9cm) lengths, bend in half to form a two-pronged pin.

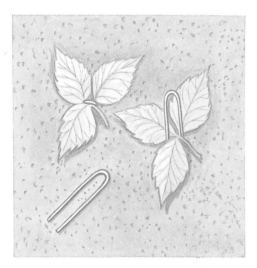

Bend a piece of wire into a U, insert into the base over a leaf or through a flower.

Bedding down

This means forming a flat, uniform surface of moss or lichen on a base or into a basket or on to a wreath using two-pronged wire pins to hold the material in place.

Wiring flowers

Fresh flowers are rarely wired nowadays except on those occasions when a wire is required to support a heavy flower head which might otherwise break off. Flowers that are to be carried or worn are wired so that the stems hold the shape into which they were designed. This also has the advantage of reducing the weight of the arrangement. Wired flower techniques are also used in dried flower work.

Spraying material

Gold and silver spray paints can be used to change the appearance of cones, seed heads, twigs etc. Mounted items can be inserted into a foam block and loose items can be placed in a large cardboard box. Shake the can well, spray and leave to dry. Turn the item and spray again to cover all the surfaces.

Spraying is best done outdoors on a windless day. It is advisable to wear disposable plastic gloves.

Varnishing

Gourds and some seed cases benefit from a coat of clear, artist's gloss varnish. A light spray with matt varnish will also seal in some grass seeds and prevent them from dropping. Varnishing will also help to prevent fragile dried material from shattering.

To preserve gourds, pierce both ends with a knitting needle, leave in a warm place to dry. You will hear the seeds rattle inside when the gourd is fully dry. Use 'Staysoft' to hold the dried gourd steady and spray one end. When dry, reverse the gourd and spray the other end.

Bunching

This term describes the gathering together of flowers, shortening the stems and then binding them with black reel wire. Two 3in (7.5cm) wire 'legs' are left so that the flowers can be mounted into foam.

Bunching flowers and binding to make 2 legs.

Bleaching

Grasses and seed heads can be bleached by laying them in a bath of domestic bleach overnight. Rinse thoroughly in clean water and hang up to dry.

Note: The strengths of the various brands of bleach on the market vary and therefore no quantities or timings can be given. Extreme care should be taken when handling bleach. Wash hands after handling containers. Keep the liquid away from clothing and furnishings. If bleach should get into the eyes or mouth, quickly dash the face with cold water and seek medical assistance immediately. Always keep bleach out of the reach of children.

SPECIALIST MATERIALS

Cones Pick these up under trees in winter or they can be obtained from some florists' suppliers and specialist shops. Kinds include cedar, Scots pine, larch and sugar pine.

Lichen In flower arranging this usually refers to reindeer moss from the arctic circle. The lichen is dyed and is useful for covering dry foam in arrangements.

Driftwood Pieces of suitable wood can sometimes be found on the seashore at low tide but driftwood is obtainable from florists' suppliers and some specialist shops.

Cork bark is another useful decorative material.

Fungus Sponge fungus and golden mushrooms have exciting shapes and textures and a wide range is usually available from florists' suppliers and specialist shops.

Gourds These can be grown from seed or you can buy them, ready-dried, from florists' suppliers.

Bun or carpet moss This is used to cover the surface of soil and gives a good finish to plant arrangements.

Twisted or tortured willow Useful and attractive bare branches which can be used in the natural state. **Tortured hazel** is also available.

Glass nuggets These are made in a range of colours and are useful for hiding florists' mechanics and as a decorative support material.

HANDLING FLOWERS
Gathering

Flowers lose their moisture on sunny days so avoid picking at midday or in the afternoon. Pick in the early evening when the sap is high and flowers can be conditioned for arranging overnight.

Take a bucket of tepid water with you. Select your flowers and cut off at a slant, using a sharp knife. Place immediately in the bucket of water, thus avoiding airlocks and any chance of wilting. Pick only what you need and cut to the stem length required.

When taking foliage, take branches from the rear of shrubs. Cut from trees as though you were pruning, in a way that will improve their shape.

Conditioning

Soft stemmed flowers With most of these, it is sufficient to cut the stems off at a slant about 1in (2.5cm) from the end of the stem with a sharp knife or scissors and plunge the stem immediately into deep, clean, tepid water so that the flower can start to draw up moisture again. Remove all leaves that will be below water level in the final arrangement.

Medium-hard stems These require to be cut at a slant, split and then have the bottom 1–2in (2.5–5cm) of bark scraped away. (Roses would be considered a medium- to hard-stemmed flower.)

Hard stems These should have the bottom 1–2in (2.5–5cm) gently crushed with a hammer.

Hollow stems Trim these with a sharp knife or scissors with the flower held upside-down. Pour water in the stem and then plug with a twist of cotton wool which will continue to allow water to be absorbed and drawn up the stem. Large delphinium and amarylis lilies come into this category.

Pour water into hollow stems, plug with cotton wool.

'Bleeding stems' Some stems emit a milky substance when cut and must be sealed to prevent the seepage congealing and forming a blockage. Sealing is done by holding the stem in a flame until the milky substance blackens and stops flowing. Examples of these flowers are poppies, euphorbia and dahlias. Some people find the substance an irritant. if it gets on to the skin it should be washed off immediately.

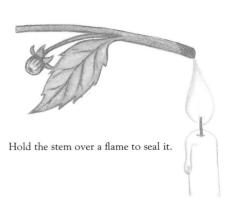

Hold the stem over a flame to seal it.

Cut medium-hard stems diagonally, split ends then scrape away the bark.

Special treatments

Some flowers require special treatment. Here are just a few of those commonly used in flower arranging.

Alium Being a member of the onion family, these flowers can smell rather unpleasant. Control this by wrapping stem ends in damp cotton wool and then sealing them in a plastic bag.

Begonia rex Plunge each leaf stem in 1in (2.5cm) of boiling water for a few seconds and then immerse the whole leaf in tepid water for about 2 hours. Take out and drain and newspaper before using.

Camellias Avoid handling the flower petals which bruise easily and turn brown at the slightest touch. Split short stems and lay the flowers on wet cotton wool.

Branches of berries Carefully strip all the leaves from a branch leaving just the berries. Crush the branch end with a hammer and immerse the entire branch in cool water for about 6 hours.

Christmas roses These are notorious for developing air locks and wilting almost immediately. Re-cut the ends then, take a sharp pin and scratch the entire length of the stem. Seal the stem in a flame and then give the flower a deep drink.

Cutting stems under alcohol.

Clematis Pour 1½in (4cm) of alcohol into a small dish and, using fine-pointed scissors, cut the stem short while it is under the surface of the alcohol. This method is used by Japanese flower arrangers.

Gladioli Slant-cut the stems with a sharp knife and remove some of the outside foliage. Pinch out the top buds.

Hydrangea Plunge stems into 1in (2.5cm) of boiling water and then float upside down in tepid water for about 3 hours. If heads show signs of wilting before the rest of a display, remove the hydrangea heads and repeat this procedure then put them back.

Lilac Strip off all the foliage, crush the stem ends and plunge them into 2in (5cm) of boiling water. Then give a deep drink.

Lilies Slant-cut the stems and remove most of the foliage. In order to prevent staining, remove the stamens before they pollinate.

Scratch the stem of a Christmas rose with a pin.

Mimosa Crush the stem ends and plunge into boiling water for 30 seconds. Give the flowers a deep, warm drink and spray the heads with a mist of water.

Stocks Remove the top buds and all the lower foliage. Gently crush the stems and give a deep drink. When stocks are used in a display the water quickly becomes unpleasant. To avoid this, daily place the container in the sink under the cold tap and allow the water to run into and overflow the container until all the water has been changed.

Tulips Remove the lower foliage, slant-cut the stems and wrap them tightly in newspaper. Plunge into deep water overnight. This will encourage the stems to stay straight. To prevent airlocks, prick through the stem under the flower head.

To prevent the stems bending, wrap tulips tightly in newspaper, stand in deep water overnight.

Violets Turn the bunches upside-down and plunge into tepid water for 1 hour before arranging them. As with hydrangeas, violets take in moisture through their petals as well as the stems.

Prolonging life
Chemical nutrient additives for prolonging the life of cut flowers are widely available and many flower arrangers have their own pet methods. Whatever aid you decide to use, a small piece of fresh charcoal will help to keep the water sweet but here are the important rules.
● Always use containers that are completely clean.
● Whichever support system you are using, use fresh clean water to start with and then top up daily. Every day, remove dead blooms and foliage and re-condition any wilting flowers.
● Avoid placing arrangements in direct sunlight, over radiators and in direct draughts.

Foliage All foliage should be cleaned and pruned to remove all damaged leaves and stems. Strip the leaves from the lower stems and the bark from the first 2in (5cm). Scrape the bark away carefully to reveal the soft, green surface underneath. Crush gently and leave the foliage in a bucket of tepid water overnight. Most foliages respond to being completely submerged in water enabling the leaves to absorb moisture but grey and silver hairy or downy leaves would be damaged by this process.

Swags of flowers and foliage have been a popular decoration for centuries. The form has also been reproduced in other mediums – the Romans embellished buildings with carved stone swags and, in the 18th century, the English sculptor and woodcarver Grinling Gibbons carved swags in fruitwoods for some of the finest interiors.

DRIED FLOWERS
Gathering
Pick stems on a dry day as soon as the dew has dried off and the sap is rising. Flowers must be in optimum condition and preferably picked before pollination has taken place. If it is necessary to pick on a damp day, gently shake the flowers and stand them in a container in 1in (2.5cm) of water until they are dry.

Remember to pick grasses also, before they go to seed and pick seedheads before they rattle. Drying takes some time so pick only as much as you can handle at one time.

Cleaning dried arrangements
Clean dust from dried arrangements with a large, soft, artist's paintbrush or use a hair dryer at its lowest setting. Hold the dryer about 12in (30cm) away from the arrangement. Use the bowl of a wooden spoon to protect any fragile pieces. Do not display dried arrangements for too long, but pack them away for a rest, and bring them out again later.

PRESERVING METHODS
Air drying
Upside-down method Fix a line or pole across an airy, warm, dark room where the flowers can be left for some time. Strip all the foliage from the flowers, arrange bunches with their heads at various levels and secure the base of the stems with a rubber band. Using a strong stub wire, bend 'S' hooks and use these to hang the bunches, heads down, from the line or pole.

Do not have too many flowers in each bunch and do not crowd bunches on the line but leave room for the air to circulate. Darkening the room will help the flowers to retain their colours.

Standing method Grasses, Chinese lanterns, sea lavender, statice and bulrushes are best dried in an upright position in a vase of dry sand. Lady's mantle and cow parsley should be started using the hanging method and, when nearly dry, transferred to a container so that they complete their drying in a more natural shape.

Hang bunches with heads down on S hooks.

Stand plants upright in a vase of dry sand.

Support drying Heavy seed heads, like globe artichokes and sweet maize, need support and extra space while drying. Stretch a piece of wire netting over a wooden frame, put it in a warm place and place the stems through the wire mesh so that the netting supports the heads.

Support heavy heads on wire netting.

Special treatments Hang large delphiniums and Bells of Ireland stems singly. Helichrysums required for use as a single head should be wired after picking and before drying. Helichrysum dried on the stem, with some of the top foliage left on, can be gathered up into a simple but quickly made bunch arrangement.

Water drying
When hydrangea and yarrow start to become 'crisp' on the plant, pick them and bring them indoors to protect the flowers from the weather. Place the stems in a container of suitable height in 1in (2.5cm) of water. Allow to dry out in a cool place and do not replenish the water.

Preserving with dessicants
A dessicant is a substance that readily takes up moisture from other materials placed near it. The ones most commonly used for drying flowers are borax, detergent powder, silica gel and silver sand.

Borax powder is perfect for fragile petals and can be dried and re-used but it is sometimes difficult to remove from the finer parts of the flowers.

Detergent powder will dry both small and large flowers but it should be used only once. Like borax, it can be difficult to remove from petals.

Silica gel This is the most expensive dessicant but it is the quickest and best one to use. It dries out quickly and can be used with flowers of all sizes. Silica gel crystals can be ground down to a fine powder to dry even the smallest flowers, so that they hold their shape.

Silver sand This works well with thicker petals and materials but it is slow-acting and can take up to three weeks. Also, it may not always remove the last traces of moisture.

Trickle silica gel from a spoon, separating the flower petals so that the crystals run between.

Dried flower arranging
Brown foam, for dried arrangements, is very lightweight. It must be securely fixed into the container and the container itself may need to be weighted, if it is to support a large display, to prevent it from overbalancing.

FLOWER AND PLANTS FOR DRYING

Air drying

Allium	Achillea
Agapanthus seedheads	Bamboo stems
Candytuft	Broom
Bells of Ireland	Cow parsley
Chinese lantern	Clary
Clematis seedheads	Cornflower
Dahlia (pompom)	Delphinium
Dock	Eucalyptus
Foxglove	Globe artichoke
Golden rod	Grasses
Gypsophila	Grape hyacinth seedheads
Heather	Helichrysum
Hogwood seedheads	Honesty
Hollyhock seedheads	Hops
Iris seedheads	Lady's mantle
Larkspur	Lavender
Love-in-a-mist seedheads	Moss
Montbretia	Love lies bleeding
Mimosa	Mugwort
Nipplewort	Pearly everlasting
Oats	Poppy seedheads
Sea holly	Sea Lavender
Shepherd's purse	Sweet William
Statice	St John's wort
Sweetcorn heads	Tansy
Teasle seedheads	Wheat
Verbena	Veronica

Water drying

Bells of Ireland	Heather
Hydrangea	Yarrow
	Larkspur

Dessicant drying

Auricula	Anemones
Buttercups	Camellias
Cornflowers	Carnations
Daffodils	Dahlias
Daisies	Delphiniums
Elderflowers	Forget-me-nots
Freesia	Gentians
Geraniums	Hellebores
Hollyhocks	Lily of the valley
Marigolds	Lilies
Orchids	Peony
Pansies	Primroses
Ranculus	Roses
Sweetpeas	Violets
Zinnias	

Preserving in glycerine

Aspidistra	Beech
Bells of Ireland	Box
Broom	Bracken
Camellia	Choisya
Cotoneaster	Eucalyptus
Fatsia	Ferns
Ivy	Laurel
Laurustinus	Lime tree flowers
Magnolia	Mahonia
Oak	Old man's beard
Pittosporum	Rhododendron
Sea holly	Sweet chestnut

Using dessicants

You need a large tin or plastic box with an airtight lid. Place a layer of dessicant in the base of the box. Cut the flower stems short to $\frac{1}{2}$in (1cm), sufficient to attach a wire after drying. Carefully lay the flowers in the dessicant, making sure that they do not touch. Using a spoon, slowly trickle dessicant amongst the petals and continue doing this until they are covered to a depth of about 1in (2.5cm). Seal on the lid.

Inspect the flowers after a few days. They are ready when they are dry and feel papery. With silica gel, the process may take only 2–4 days.

If left too long, the flowers dry out and become too fragile to handle.

Carefully pour off the dessicant into another container and pick out the flowers, one at a time, as they come to the surface. Lay them on a plate or tray. Carefully brush any remaining dessicant from the petals with an artist's soft paint brush.

Turn the flowers upside down on soft, folded muslin and glue on false wire stems and then carefully cover the wire with stem tape.

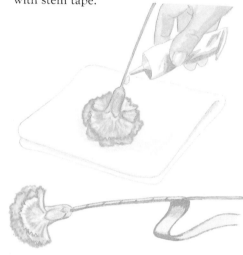

Place dried flower on soft fabric, glue on a wire stem, cover the stem with tape.

Depending on the type of foliage, it will take between 1 and 4 weeks for the

Stand branches in a jar of glycerine mixture, put the jar in a bucket.

Pour glycerine mixture over single leaves in a shallow dish.

Preserving with glycerine

Glycerine is mostly used for preserving foliage. It will change the colours of leaves to shades of brown but they will retain their suppleness. Unlike dried material, foliage preserved in this way is not easily damaged.

Make up a mixture of 60% glycerine to 40% hot water. Pour the liquid into a glass jar and put the jar into a large container (such as a bucket). Strip the lower foliage from the branches and scrape the bark from the bottom 2in (5cm) of the stem. Crush the ends with a hammer and put the stems into the jar so that the bucket rim supports the branches.

leaves to be preserved. You will be able to tell by the look and feel of the leaves when they are ready.

To preserve individual leaves, use a 50/50 mixture of glycerine and hot water. Place the leaves in a shallow dish and cover with the solution. Push the leaves down into the mixture from time to time. They should be ready in a few days. Lift out, wash in soapy water, spread on folded newspaper and pat dry.

Making a garland or wreath

Cut a piece of wire netting to the required length and to about 12in (30cm) wide. (If you are making a wreath, lay a circle of string to the diameter you want, then measure it.)

Lay the netting on a flat surface. Make a mound of damp sphagnum moss along the edge nearest to you.

Roll the wire netting away from you and over the moss to form a roll. For a swag or garland, fold in the ends. For a wreath, bend the tube ends round until they touch, then 'sew' together with black reel wire. If the garland or wreath is to be used for dried material, leave it to dry before working on it.

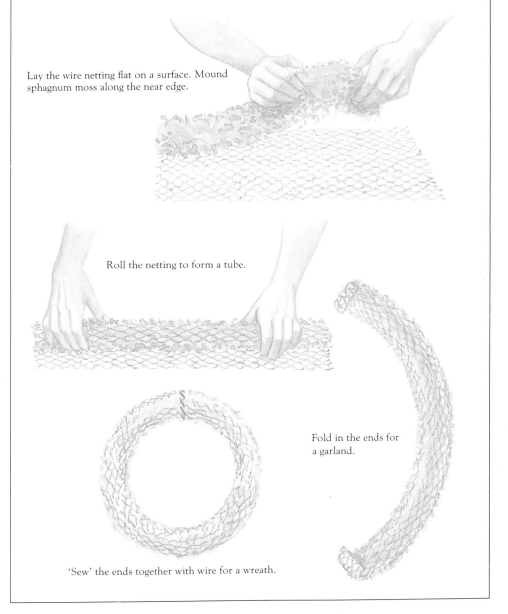

Lay the wire netting flat on a surface. Mound sphagnum moss along the near edge.

Roll the netting to form a tube.

Fold in the ends for a garland.

'Sew' the ends together with wire for a wreath.

Ribbon bows

The water-resistant ribbon obtainable from florists is the easiest to work with but polyester satin ribbon can also be used. Form a length of ribbon into a figure-of-eight, holding the centre between thumb and forefinger. With the same length of ribbon make another figure-of-eight, holding the bows together at the centre. Bind the two bows together with a lightweight stub wire, leaving two mounting 'legs'. If you find making this method difficult, mount single loops and insert several in the same place.

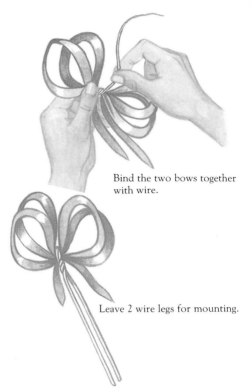

Bind the two bows together with wire.

Leave 2 wire legs for mounting.

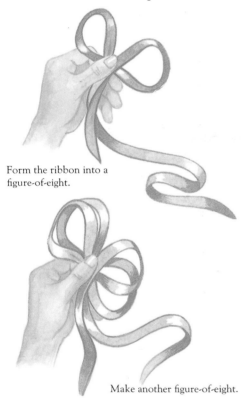

Form the ribbon into a figure-of-eight.

Make another figure-of-eight.

Paper bows

Untwist 3yd (2.75m) of paper ribbon rope. Make a small 2in (5cm) loop and bind tightly with reel wire. Make a second loop, slightly larger, and bind again. Continue making loops of increasing size, binding each one tightly at the same position. Leave the last length of ribbon straight. Twist the reel wire ends together tightly leaving two 'legs'.

Swirls can be added by cutting narrow lengths of ribbon and wrapping the strips round a pencil. Pull out the pencil, attach a mounting wire and add the swirls to the centre of the bow.

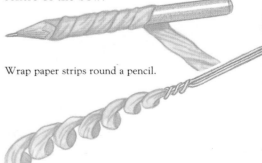

Wrap paper strips round a pencil.

Remove the pencil and attach a mounting wire.

Quick-drying glue

There are several good, clear adhesives on the market which are ideal for flower work. Glue guns are expensive but quick and clean to handle. Hot-melt stick refills are used with glue guns and electric power is needed.

Ribbon bows for you to try
Rosette
Loop the ribbon as shown, tie in the middle with another piece of ribbon. Spread out the loops. Fish-tail the ribbon ends. This design can also be turned into a star by cutting the loops and fish-tailing the ends.

Make more figures-of-eight and add them, laying them first one way, then the other until a chrysanthemum has been formed. You need about 14 circles to get the effect.

Rosette

Daisy bow
This works best with cut-edge gift ribbon. Cut 4 pieces about 8in (20cm) long. Lay the pieces in a star shape. Stick at the centre with glue. Bring up the ends and glue together, to make a ball. Dab glue inside and then push the top and bottom together firmly until they stick.

Chrysanthemum bow

Flat bow
Cut a strip of cut-edge ribbon and bring the ends together. Stick the ends to the middle with glue. Make a slightly smaller bow in the same way and stick on top of the first. Make a third, smaller bow and stick on top of the second. Cut a short strip of ribbon and bind round the three joined bows.

Flat bow

Daisy bow

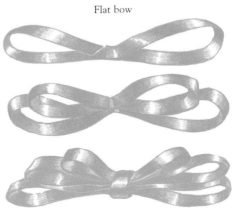

Chrysanthemum bow
Cut ½in (1cm)-wide cut-edge ribbon into 16in (40cm) lengths. Stick the strip ends together to form circles. Twist the circles into figures-of-eight, dab glue to hold the shape. Join 2 figures-of-eight with glue.

111

Acknowledgements

Blooms of Bressingham Ltd
Bressingham, Diss, Norfolk, IP22 2AB
for plants, shrubs and conifers.

Swan Craft Gallery
Ashfield cum Thorpe,
Stowmarket, Suffolk, IP14 6LU
for dried flowers, floral material
and flower mechanics. Send a
stamped, self-addressed envelope
for information and prices.

Linda Grey for hellebores and globe artichokes.

All designs in this book are the author's own.